Original title:
Through the Tropical Heat

Copyright © 2025 Creative Arts Management OÜ
All rights reserved.

Author: Miriam Kensington
ISBN HARDBACK: 978-1-80581-609-6
ISBN PAPERBACK: 978-1-80581-136-7
ISBN EBOOK: 978-1-80581-609-6

Land of the Emerald Breeze

In a land where sweat drips down,
And the sun wears a blazing crown,
Lizards dance, they sure know how,
To keep cool in the heat, oh wow!

Coconuts fall with a thud,
As I trip in the warm, soft mud,
The palm trees sway, they mock my strut,
While I search for shade, just my luck!

Mangoes ripen, they start to shout,
"Eat me now, or I'll pout!"
I take a bite, juice all around,
Bees start buzzing, it's a madhouse sound!

The locals laugh, they have a feast,
Fish tacos, oh, what a treat!
But here I am, with sunburned feet,
In this wild joy, I'm feeling beat!

Delights of the Steamy Dawn

Morning sun is blazing bright,
Sweaty brows in the soft light.
Lizards dance, what a sight,
Chasing flies with all their might.

Coffee drips, oh what a thrill,
Taste so strong, can make you chill.
Rooster crows, what a loud quill,
Sipping slow, we bend to will.

Colorful Trails Beyond the Tropics

Breezy paths of bright delight,
Mangoes rolling, what a bite!
Birds are singing, oh so spry,
Dodging sunbeams in the sky.

Frogs jump high in joyful glee,
Chasing shadows, feeling free.
Coconuts fall like laughter loud,
Every day, we're feeling proud.

Embrace of the Serene Night

Starry skies with twinkling cheer,
Crickets chirp, the end is near.
Mosquitoes buzzing, what a show,
Waving hands, come on, let's go!

Fireflies dancing in the air,
Flickering lights, I swear they care.
Tropical breeze, all's not quite right,
But we'll laugh till the morning light.

Whispers of the Clairvoyant Sea

Waves tell secrets, soft and sweet,
With every splash, they skip a beat.
Shells are giggling, what a tease,
Breezy laughter, brings such ease.

Floating thoughts on foam and tide,
Spinning dreams we can't confide.
Salty air, a silly grin,
With every wave, the fun begins.

The Flare of Blossoms Unfurling

In the garden, colors clash,
Petals dancing, quite a splash.
Bees are buzzing, oh so loud,
While I seek a comfy cloud.

Lizards leap with comic flair,
Chasing shadows without a care.
Sunshine turns my skin to toast,
Giving jokes from coast to coast.

Thirsty plants do stand and sway,
While I sip a drink all day.
Sweaty brows and silly hats,
Even ducks wear tiny spats.

Beneath the Hibiscus Blooms

A cat in shade, so sly and slick,
Pauses under blooms, a trick!
Butterflies with painted wings,
Flirt around like joyous kings.

Watermelons rolling near,
Slipping, sliding, oh dear, fear!
A picnic crew in wild delight,
Snacks that vanish out of sight.

Waves of laughter swell and rise,
As ants march in a line— oh my!
Grinning fruits with faces bright,
All escaping from the bite.

Elysian Echoes of Heat Waves

Echoes pulse with silly cheer,
Heat waves dance, my nose is near.
Frogs in shades, they hold a chat,
While the sun makes me feel flat.

Chickens frolic, strut with ease,
Stirring up their feathery tease.
Popsicles melting, what a race,
Chasing ice with windy grace.

Laughter floats like scented air,
As umbrellas spread everywhere.
Sunburnt noses tell a tale,
Of wacky winks and sunbeam whale.

Rhythms of the Sultry Air

In sultry air, we twist and twirl,
Dancing 'round like dizzy whirl.
Coconut drinks all around,
Making muddy footprints on the ground.

The breeze whispers sweet, soft jokes,
As mangoes drop with silly pokes.
Palm trees sway, creating beats,
While the sun sneaks tasty treats.

Bikini clowns parade with flair,
Balancing drinks while losing hair.
Every moment bursts with fun,
Laughing hard at day's bright run.

The Siren Call of Nightfall

The sun goes down, the crickets sing,
The frogs all join in, what a fling!
Mosquitoes ready for a midnight snack,
While we wonder if we'll make it back.

The fireflies dance in blurry lines,
Winking at us with their glowing signs.
We wave our arms like silly fools,
Dodging the bugs, breaking all the rules.

Devotion in the Steamy Air

The weather's hotter than Auntie May,
Her casserole from yesterday!
Sweat drips down like a river wide,
As we sip on drinks that just slide.

Bikini season, oh what a sight,
A beach ball's flying, oh what a flight!
But do not ask me to play a game,
I'll just stick here, it's way too lame.

Tales from the Thundering Storm

Raindrops tumble, splatters galore,
Smiling in puddles, who could ask for more?
Lightning flashes, a bright parade,
While we seek shelter, umbrellas betrayed.

Our clothes are drenched, hair's a mess,
Lightning bolts dance, such a stress!
But laughter echoes through the rain,
As we splash like kids, again and again.

A Canvas of Bitter and Sweet

Fruity drinks in the blazing sun,
A mix of flavors, it's such fun!
Tropical fruits with a hint of sass,
One too many, I might just pass.

The coconut falls with a booming thud,
Splashing in water, a watery flood.
Yet here I sit, with a silly grin,
Summer's a blast, let the good times begin!

Opalescent Glimmers at Noon

The sun's a disco ball, so bright,
Sweating birds take off in flight.
A lizard does a funky dance,
While ants all tailor a merry chance.

Palm trees sway to the sun's loud tune,
With leaves that shimmer, claiming June.
A coconut drops, a quirky thud,
As squirrels gather and form a flood.

Sweaty hats bob on heads like boats,
While flip-flops flip, lost in their coats.
And laughter bubbles, light and clear,
As sunshine tickles the nearby deer.

The day unfolds with a silly twist,
Even the frogs can't resist the mist.
In this warm soup, joy reigns supreme,
A sunlit party, a sun-soaked dream.

Boiling Skies and Soft Horizons

Under the sun, it's quite a sight,
The bees wear shades, feeling just right.
Lemonade rivers flow down the street,
Where popsicles dribble with summertime heat.

A hammock waits, like a fluffy cloud,
As folks lie back, relaxed and loud.
The sun's embrace isn't too polite,
It aims straight for toes, a warm delight.

Glaciers of ice in glasses clink,
While watermelon boats sail down in sync.
A rubber duck starts a wild parade,
As giggles erupt in fresh lemonade.

Up above, the kites take flight,
Painting the sky in colors so bright.
It's a boiling day, but who can complain?
When laughter is loud, and fun is the gain.

Rustling Dreams in the Leafy Shade

In the shade, where the breezes play,
Squirrels gossip and dance away.
An umbrella drinks up the sun's hot rays,
As laughter hides in leafy bays.

A picnic spreads like a patchwork quilt,
With cookies crumbling, but no guilt.
The ants are plotting a sneaky heist,
While sandwiches steal the sunshine's feast.

The butterflies wear tuxedos quite bold,
As ice cream drips and stories unfold.
Tangled limbs turn shy as they snack,
Laughter rustles down the leafy track.

The sunbeams flicker like a joyous tune,
Tickling all in a sparkling swoon.
Hide from the sun, not from the cheer,
Fun in the shade as the world draws near.

Hidden Trails of Pearly Light

In the garden, shadows wiggle and glance,
Where daisies lead a curious dance.
The rays peek in, a playful tease,
While hidden paths invite the breeze.

Mango trees wear funny hats,
As squirrels make their daring spats.
A hidden stream hums a gentle song,
Where pebbles giggle, and time feels wrong.

Fireflies twirl in evening's go,
While frogs croak out a silly show.
They leap with zest, a talent unique,
As crickets chirp their comical speak.

A moonbeam laughs, lighting the way,
In this enchanting, whimsical play.
Twilight glimmers, a soft delight,
On hidden trails of pearly light.

Somewhere Between Heat and Harmony

In the jungle, sweat beads form,
A dance with mosquitoes, far from warm.
Flip-flops clash on the vibrant ground,
While crazy toucans squawk all around.

Pineapple hats upon our heads,
Dreams of ice cream fill our beds.
Lizards laughing, sunning tight,
Finding shade is quite the fight.

Coconuts rolling down the street,
Hiccups caused by spicy treats.
The sun's a tease with a wink and grin,
August afternoons—let the games begin!

Bouncing balls in the air so bright,
With every splash, we feel delight.
Sand between toes, laughter so fleet,
In this madness, we find our beat.

Revelations Among the Vines

Amid the vines, a grape takes flight,
Whispering secrets 'til the night.
Climbing high, my friend takes a tumble,
Rolling in laughter, oh what a jumble!

A parrot's gossip, a monkey's chant,
Dancing under the stars, let's plant.
Bananas slide under careful feet,
As laughter echoes on this sweet beat.

Fruits debating who's the finest,
Avocados claiming they're the kindest.
Papaya winks, "I'm best for a grin,"
But everyone knows it's the melon's win!

Between the vines, we stop to play,
Swapping stories, come what may.
In this lush maze, silliness reigns,
As we sip drinks through funny refrains.

Surging Currents of the Sunkissed Soul.

Waves of sun dance on my nose,
As I chase after a giant hose.
Splashing wildly, I lose my grip,
Grinning wide in this goofy trip.

Seagulls steal fries without a care,
Aerial acrobats roaming the air.
Sandcastles crumble, but who's to mind?
In this hot chaos, joy is what we find.

Lemonade spills like wild confetti,
As we beat the heat, feeling quite petty.
Giggling fish jump near my toes,
This sun-kissed day hilariously flows.

In salty air, we sing our song,
With overly tan friends, we all belong.
Underneath the sky so blue,
Fueling our laughter, just me and you.

Beneath the Searing Sun

Beneath the rays, we brave the heat,
With sun hats large and sticky feet.
Ice cream dribbles down our chins,
As we laugh about our silly sins.

Cactus winks at a blooming flower,
Braving the sun with all its power.
Bugs play tag on a sizzling chair,
In this hot mess, no one seems to care.

Sunscreen battles on our dryish skin,
Pranking each other with a cheeky grin.
Sipping coconut, we cheer for fun,
Counting the ways to dash from the sun.

With every hiccup, friendship grows,
In this summery madness, the laughter flows.
The beach is calling, our hearts so light,
Under the burning sky so bright.

Fastened by the Rhythms of Life

In the jungle, a monkey swings,
Chasing shadows, he laughs and sings.
The parrot squawks a silly tune,
While the sun bakes us like a croon.

A lizard darts, slick as ice,
He winks at me, oh, what a vice!
We dance to beats of a froggy band,
Playing in a swamp so wonderfully grand.

Pineapple hats on heads of fools,
Fruits grow wild in the sunny schools.
A slip on leaves, laughter in air,
Oh, life is a circus, without a care!

Bamboo sticks for silly swords,
Fighting off imaginary hordes.
Life here is bright, a comical spree,
Under the sun, oh, just let it be!

Rain-soaked Dreams and Kisses

A dance in puddles, splash so high,
Umbrella's flipped – oh my, oh my!
The storm clouds gather, but who's upset?
We're soaking wet, as if in a pet.

Rubber ducks parade in a line,
Floating past with a hint of brine.
We splash and slide on streets so slick,
Laughing loudly, it's quite the trick!

Kisses in raindrops, sweet like pie,
Wind tousles hair as we twirl and fly.
The thunder claps a jealous cheer,
Celebrate chaos, with giggles near!

With every drop, our worries fade,
In this wet world, no plans are made.
Just raindrop dreams and cheeky bliss,
In puddles deep, we steal a kiss!

Blossoms of Exuberance and Spices

Rosemary whispers to minty sage,
In the garden of giggles, life's the stage.
The sun shines bright on the flavorful crew,
Mixing herbs like a giant stew!

Chili peppers giggle, oh so hot,
While basil winks in its green little spot.
Lavender dances, sweet perfume wafts,
As we toss spices, creating our crafts.

A marigold jumps, wearing a crown,
Flipping and twisting, never a frown.
We plant our laughter, watch it grow,
With joy in our hearts, the seeds we sow!

Honey bees buzz their curious tunes,
While crickets chirp under the moons.
Flavors collide, a zesty delight,
In this silly garden, all feels right!

Ephemeral Moments Under the Moon

The night sky giggles with twinkling stars,
While a raccoon sings from behind the bars.
The moon's a balloon, round and bright,
As we dance like fools, under its light.

Fireflies flash their tiny bling,
Inviting all creatures to join and sing.
The banana peels make for slick slides,
Impromptu races, where laughter abides.

Cupcakes of dreams, frosting on top,
We munch and crunch, and never stop.
In this silly moment, time stands still,
Chasing shadows, it's a joy-filled thrill!

Stars wink at us, as if to say,
Embrace the night, let worries stray.
With giggles echoing, hearts in tune,
We'll revel in madness, under the moon!

Secrets of the Sultry Night

Beneath the stars, the mosquitoes dance,
Whispers of secrets in every glance.
Laughter erupts as they play the fool,
Tripping over shadows, oh, what a duel!

The frogs croak tunes, the crickets compete,
While locals parade in shorts and bare feet.
Tropical breezes bring air so sweet,
Adding a bounce to the night's heartbeat.

The Sweat of Summer Bliss

Oh, how we glisten on this sunny day,
Like melting ice cream, we slowly sway.
Our shirts may stick, our jokes never fail,
Each laugh is a splash; we're left to flail!

Watermelon drips run down our chin,
In this sticky mess, let the fun begin.
With every bite, we giggle and grin,
A fruity sticky summer, where chaos wins!

Lush Canopies and Hidden Paths

Beneath green leaves, adventure awaits,
We stumble through, laughing at our fates.
Branches low hanging like a tricky test,
"Dodge this one!" we yell; it's a jungle fest!

Veering left, we find a muddy stream,
With a splash and a laugh, it's just like a dream.
Our shoes are lost, but we don't mind the mess,
With nature's embrace, we're feeling blessed!

Swaying to the Rhythm of Rain

The pitter-patter sings a silly tune,
Rain drops boogie, much like a loon.
Umbrellas flip like pancakes, oh dear,
Laughter erupts as we twirl without fear!

Dancing puddles splash rhythmically right,
As we slide and glide in the soft moonlight.
Soaked to the skin, we're a sight to see,
In this dance of joy, we're completely free!

Fleeing Clouds and Summer Swim

The sun blazes down, oh what a sight,
Squirrels dance around, in sheer delight.
Umbrellas flop like fish out of the sea,
While folks forget their woes, sipping iced tea.

A beach ball drifts, with no one to chase,
A dog steals a towel, what a funny case!
Flip-flops are flying with no sense of aim,
As laughter erupts, it's a wacky game.

Children build castles that quickly collapse,
Seagulls swoop in, plotting silly mishaps.
The lifeguard's on break, lost in a snack,
While sunscreen flies, making quite the track.

Now as the day fades, all hues really pop,
We pack up the laughter, as we hop, hop, hop.
Just don't lose your flip-flops, or your ice cream too,
For whimsical mischief is waiting for you!

The Sweetness of Overripe Mangoes

Mangoes seductive, on a sunlit day,
Juices drip down like a foolish ballet.
Sticky fingers wave, oh what a scene,
As laughter erupts like a bubbling sheen.

A fruit truck rolls in, causing a stir,
The crowd goes wild, oh what a blur!
Mango pits fly like boomerangs bold,
While grandma just giggles, her secrets unfold.

Tropical vibes in a fruit-filled craze,
Fruits become hats for the sunniest plays.
Sipping smoothies like pirates at sea,
Who knew such a mess could be so carefree?

As dusk settles in, with a mango encore,
Their sweetness still lingers, who could want more?
With faces sticky and wide grins so bright,
We relish the chaos, it feels just right!

Untamed Spirits of the Shoreline

Waves crash and tumble, a wild surprise,
Surfboards and giggles fill up the skies.
A beach bonfire? No, just a hot dog,
As laughter echoes, a mysterious fog.

Shells tumble down, like forgotten jokes,
Sandcastles crumble as seagulls poke.
Picnics gone rogue, ants all around,
We dance in a circle, stumbling on ground.

Flip-flops in hand, we race for the sea,
Splashing like dolphins, all wild and free.
A sunburned nose—who would have guessed?
The shore is alive, our silly fest.

As stars twinkle down, we gather as one,
Stories and laughter spill, oh what fun!
With hearts like children and spirits so bright,
We celebrate chaos into the night!

Currents of a Tropical Heartbeat

A hammock sways, in the warm, sweet breeze,
While coconut crabs practice ballet with ease.
Cool drinks in hand, let giggles erupt,
As we try to dance, and hilariously interrupt.

The sunset paints us in colors absurd,
Like clowns in a circus, oh haven't you heard?
With beach games that fail, and belly laughs rise,
We chase after kites, under painted skies.

Palm trees shake hands, in a playful whirl,
As we twirl and twist, oh what a swirl!
Sand in our toes, and joy in our hearts,
This vibrant rhythm, no one departs.

And when evening falls, our tales turn to gold,
Every chuckle a treasure, forever retold.
With waves as our soundtrack, we sway and we play,
In this wild, wacky world, come what may!

The Heat of a Thousand Stars

In the sun, my ice cream melts,
Drips down my hand, oh how it quenches,
I chase the thrills of sunburned pelts,
As bees decide to join my clenches.

The flip-flops squeak, my feet are bare,
Each step a dance on sizzling ground,
I wonder if my socks are there,
Or did they flee, not wanting to drown?

The shade is prime, but whoa, beware!
The neighbor's cat, an acrobat,
Leaps in my lap with sunbeam flair,
So now I've got a furry hat!

But plastic chairs just heat my seat,
A sauna made of cushy foam,
I stand to stamp my sandy feet,
And hum a tune to find my home.

Solstice Sorrows and Joys

The sun blares down with grand delight,
I step outside – it's like a fry!
Sweaty brows, but smiles are bright,
Who needs a gym? We stretch to dry.

The squirrels on limbs just stare at me,
I'm rigged with chips, they plot their heist,
As lemonade drips down with glee,
A toast to summer, oh so nice!

The pool's a puddle, oh my grief,
An inflatable flamingo, oh so grand,
I slip and slide like comic relief,
As friends all laugh and lend a hand.

I pull the hose, I squirt and run,
Water fights that end with shrieks,
In the season's heat, it's all just fun,
We dance on grass, a day unique!

Hummingbird's Serenade

A hum, a buzz, the garden's song,
Tiny wings in frenetic flight,
As flowers sway, they can't go wrong,
While I sip tea, wrapped up tight.

The sun beats down with no retreat,
Yet blooms are bold and colors gleam,
I find a shade, I claim my seat,
And watch the birds fulfill their dream.

A spaghetti dance of sunlit fliers,
They sip from vines as sugar spills,
While I just sit and feel the fires,
Of sunshine buzzing in my thrills.

So here I lounge, sunblushed and free,
While moths find snacks in my old hat,
If butterflies can shimmy by me,
I'll keep this heat and love the chat!

Secrets of the Banana Leaves

Beneath the fan of green delight,
The dapper lizards strut their best,
They think they are the kings of night,
While I just crave a cozy rest.

The bananas grin, they know my mood,
The wrinkled leaves sway soft and low,
As I dive into a fruity brood,
Atop a hammock's rhythmic flow.

I swear those fruits have plans, you see,
They wriggle in the market's sun,
They make me feel like quite the spree,
Each bite a giggle, oh what fun!

The jungle whispers secrets sweet,
Of parties held in twilight's sun,
I laugh aloud, can't feel my feet,
In tropic giggles, we just run!

A Dance with Monsoon Breezes

The raindrops tap a silly beat,
While frogs start their own drum retreat.
Umbrellas flip like giant sails,
As laughter swirls in wind-blown trails.

Are those clouds or cotton candy?
The sun peeks out, a bit too dandy.
Puddles leap with a splashy cheer,
While wet socks dance without a fear.

Spin in circles, feet all a-splash,
We'll take on this deluge in a dash.
With every drop, we shout hooray,
Who knew a storm could be so play?

The skies get dark, but we won't fret,
For every storm, we're the best duet.
Let thunder rumble, let lightning strike,
In this funny dance, we feel so alike.

Whispering Palms of Paradise

The palms sway in a breezy jest,
They whisper secrets, quite the quest.
One shakes hands with a vibing breeze,
While another giggles at what it sees.

A coconut plops, a thud on the head,
"Who rolled this boulder?" a traveler said.
But laughter sprouts from tropic gales,
As everyone shares their fruit-filled tales.

Sunshine tickles with its golden touch,
"Is that such a tickle, or am I just much?"
With sunglasses on, I join the crew,
A dance with the leaves, oh, what a view!

In this lush realm, we feel sweet grace,
Sun-kissed cheeks and laughter in place.
The palms will sway, and so will we,
In our paradise, forever free.

Ember Skies and Ocean Tides

Sunset spills colors with a grin,
Like painter's swirls, where fun begins.
The ocean jokes in bubbly waves,
"Surf's up, humans! Come see what braves!"

Flip-flops flying, what a sight,
Sand stuck between toes, pure delight.
The tide teases the shoreline's reach,
While crabs in costumes play on the beach.

With bonfire crackles, stories ignite,
Ghost tales told under starry height.
"Did you see that one?" as embers dance,
"She just floated by! Must be a chance!"

The evening hums like a playful tune,
As laughter twinkles beneath the moon.
In this world where skies are wide,
Life's a ride, come take the tide!

Sunlit Caress on Skin

The sun arrives with a cheeky grin,
Warming our hearts, a playful win.
Sunscreen battles, slippery spree,
"Hurry, dear friend, don't burn like me!"

Sandcastles built with artistic flair,
"Watch out! That wave's a cheeky bear!"
As buckets splash and shovels fly,
We giggle at clouds passing by.

Coconut drinks with shades so bright,
Sipping slowly, what a sight!
The ice cubes dance like little fawns,
Laughing with us till the dawn.

The sun dips low, we wave goodbye,
To this warm world where we can't be shy.
With our fun memories, we'll take a spin,
Where every day's a sunlit win!

Fires of Daybreak

The sun pops up like toast,
Setting palm trees ablaze,
Sweaty brows raise the most,
As we greet the sunny craze.

Chickens go clucking mad,
Dancing to the morning tune,
While I sip my drink, oh glad,
That I'm not a sunbaked raccoon.

Humidity takes a bow,
And my shirt sticks like glue,
With every step, I say wow,
That's a sauna for a shoe!

So let's hike in shades of green,
Laughing at the blazing rays,
Wishing for some ice cream,
In this oven of sunny days.

Songs of Night

As twilight wraps in gold,
The crickets start their show,
In this concert, oh so bold,
They steal the spotlight, you know.

A mosquito's tune arises,
As it buzzes near my ear,
I swat it with weird surprises,
"Is nature always this clear?"

Fireflies dance with glee,
Their glow like tiny lamps,
I trip over a root, oh me,
In the land of nighttime champs!

With laughter in the air,
And shadows playing tricks,
I hike beyond my compare,
Counting stars with silly flicks.

The Aroma of Overripe Limes

In the grove where limes fall,
A fruity scent invades,
Does the fruit have a call?
Surprise! It's lime charades.

I slipped on a citrus round,
On this slippery delight,
Like a clown I hit the ground,
Garlic cloves had a bite!

Bees buzz with a juicy plan,
Ignoring my sunburned face,
While I dance like a madman,
With a lime-flavored grace.

So, here in this zesty plight,
With laughter and squeeze, we cheer,
Let's toast under the moonlight,
To our funny, fruity beer!

Turquoise Waters and Whispered Hues

The ocean's calling my name,
In turquoise, pure delight,
Waves bring a playful game,
And sunscreen's my fashion rite.

I dive in, what a splash,
A fish swims by, oh dear,
It's gone in a coral flash,
Guess it gets the last frontier!

Floating on a rubber duck,
With sunglasses far too bright,
I wave at a passing truck,
In this watery sunset light.

Every splash like giggling waves,
Cheeky seagulls perched above,
In stories of sunlit braves,
This beach was made for love!

Surreal Colors in the Blazing Sun

Sunburned toes dance on hot sand,
I'm an odd artistic mess,
With ice cream in hand, not planned,
Melting dreams in summer's dress.

Umbrellas bloom like flowers,
In shades of pink and lime,
While I chase the sunny hours,
Like a kid in a candy chime.

Hat on my head, tilted askew,
Sunglasses warped like funhouse glaze,
Life's a quirky cartoon view,
In this beachside daze of rays.

With laughter splashed all around,
And ketchup on my face,
In this vibrant, wild playground,
Blazing fun in every place.

In the Arms of the Summer Breeze

The sun's a giant, blazing pie,
With sweat beads racing down my thigh.
A squirrel's dance on a sunlit beam,
Makes me question what's a dream.

Flip-flops slapping, laughter rings,
As ants prepare for their grand flings.
A coconut rolls, a perfect score,
While I'm left guessing what's in store.

In this sauna, I sip my drink,
Guzzle it fast, then pause to think.
The world's a grill, I'm feeling fried,
Best find shade or I'll be denied.

There's joy in this sticky mess of cheer,
Melting like ice cream, oh dear, oh dear!
But I'll embrace this golden plight,
In the summer's arms, everything's alright.

Exploration on Heated Paths

I wandered off on a sunny spree,
Found my hat clinging to a tree.
A lizard grinned, 'Hey, want to play?'
As I tripped over a rogue bouquet.

The path was hot, a molten lane,
Where flip-flops squeaked like they're in pain.
I met a frog with a croaky jest,
'This is no sauna, but it's a quest.'

A buzzard squawked, a wise old sage,
'Why sweat like that? Turn the page!'
I laughed aloud, feeling quite daft,
'You'll soon see why I'm on this craft.'

Roasting with glee, I embraced my quest,
Chasing my dreams in this toasty jest.
In every drip of sweat, a delight,
This heated adventure, oh, what a sight!

Mysteries Beneath the Banyan

Under the shade of roots so wide,
A monkey swings, takes me for a ride.
With giggles echoing all around,
I ponder what secrets in shade abound.

The breeze tickles, a playful tease,
While whispers flutter like playful bees.
A beetle strutted in fancy shoes,
'Beat that,' he grinned, 'you've got to choose!'

I searched for treasure, but found a shoe,
Along with a sandwich, half-eaten too.
In this jungle of laughter and cheer,
Each mystery hides a story dear.

Yet as the sun winks, I must flee,
Laughing at antics of life's spree.
In the depths of the banyan's embrace,
I find humor in this wacky space.

Quietude Amidst the Canopy

In leafy realms where the parrots squawk,
I sip my drink, take a leisurely talk.
A sloth hangs low, a lazy sight,
While I'm racing thoughts with all my might.

The trees giggle as they sway, so free,
'There's no rush here, just you and me!'
Yet as I ponder what life should be,
A gecko jived, 'Just chill with glee!'

I tried to meditate, be oh-so-still,
But a mosquito buzzed, a tiny thrill.
It danced around, a circus star,
And made me question why I travel far.

In the canopy's cloak, I find my peace,
With each fluttering leaf, laughter won't cease.
In nature's giggle, I feel the light,
Quietude wraps me, everything's right.

Embrace of the Humid Breeze

Sweat beads dance upon my brow,
Chasing shadows, oh how they bow.
A lizard grins, sunbathing proud,
While I look like a dripping cloud.

Flip-flops flop in a comical race,
My hair's a mess, what a wild chase!
The sun's a prankster, bright and bold,
Making every ice cream cone untold.

In this sauna, I laugh and sing,
Embracing all the heat waves bring.
A parrot squawks, it mocks my plight,
But I'll roast marshmallows in daylight!

With sunburns as badges, we strut and pose,
In a paradise where everyone glows.
So here's to fun in the sticky air,
With sticky laughs that fill the square.

Echoes of the Coconut Grove

Underneath the swaying trees,
Coconuts drop with a comical ease.
I dodge and duck with each loud thud,
Trying not to slip on the muddy crud.

The monkeys laugh, they steal my drink,
While I ponder life and how to think.
With sticky hands, I juggle dreams,
As a passing squirrel laughs at my schemes.

A breeze tickles my nose and cheeks,
And suddenly, the laughter peaks.
Tropical fruits rolling like balls,
While I trip over my own two stalls.

In the grove of giggles, the sun plays tricks,
A dance of shadows, a game of flicks.
So let's toast to this silly spree,
Where laughter blooms, oh so carefree.

Mirage of Flames and Ferns

The sun's a furnace, my skin's so pink,
Every thought I had just starts to sink.
I wave to a cactus, quite confused,
It's grinning back, advice misused.

A gecko jogs, with speed divine,
While I'm sweating buckets of lemon-lime.
Ferns here wink, fanning out laughs,
As I recount my roasting gaffes.

Mirages dance in the sultry air,
Promises of lemonade, sweets to share.
Instead, I find a giant bug,
As I sit on a warm forest rug.

With beads of salt and a cheeky grin,
I toast my brain for what's about to spin.
So here's to paradise, absurd and fine,
Where every sunburn feels like sunshine.

Fluttering Palms in the Dusk

As evening falls, the palms start to sway,
Dancing shadows in a light ballet.
I join the rhythm, doing my best,
While mosquitoes cheer, I stand addressed.

The beach ball rolls, what a silly sight,
I chase it down with all my might.
Sand sticks to me like an old friend,
But in this mess, I laugh till the end.

A crab scuttles, with a wink and a nod,
It's my dance partner, oh how odd!
With coconuts dangling, we spin on sand,
Making memories, hand in hand.

In the dusk's embrace, let's giggle away,
With palm fronds fluttering, let's play and sway.
Where laughter and fun never seem to die,
In this tropical laughter, we'll always fly.

Glimmers of Tropical Magic

Whispers dance on breezy nights,
A sweat-soaked shirt, oh what a sight!
Lizards lounge, wearing sunny grins,
While I search for where the cool breeze spins.

Coconuts wobble like heads in trance,
As I attempt an awkward dance.
How do umbrellas take flight so bold?
In this heat, they must be made of gold!

My ice cream dreams melt, it's true,
Sticky fingers, a sweet rendezvous.
Parrots gossip from the palm tree's perch,
About my sunscreen, they all research!

The hammock's calling, but so is the sun,
A tug of war, who will have more fun?
A crab scuttles past, in a hurry to flee,
As I contemplate, is the ocean for me?

Ray of Sun on Drenched Rocks

A sunbeam strikes, it takes its aim,
My forehead's now a sauna game.
Flip-flops squeak on a squishy floor,
Can't tell if it's a beach or a chore!

Crabs have better manners, I soon learn,
As I slip and slide, filled with concern.
My towel waves like a flag in war,
While sunscreen's fighting a mighty score.

I spot a coconut, I'm on a quest,
Too bad it bounces, causing unrest.
Seagulls laugh like they own the place,
Chiming in at my sun-soaked disgrace.

The sea calls softly, yet oh so sly,
As I ponder life's great supply.
Will I ever be cool? Only time can tell,
For every splash brings a sunburned yell!

Hidden Oceans Under Blazing Skies

Beneath the rays, adventures stir,
Like mermaids hidden, all in a blur.
Floating fish wear their finest bling,
While I manage to trip over everything.

A friendly crab waves, his name is Fred,
Does he mind if I rest my head?
The ocean laughs, rumbles with glee,
As I wonder if it would swallow me.

Jellyfish disco lights surround,
As I flail about, trying not to drown.
"Lifeguard, I'm here! Just taking a dip!"
But it seems my flip-flops are my own trip!

The sun sets low, casting shadows wide,
I join a conch in an evening slide.
We'll swap our stories of the day's mishaps,
While the moon giggles and the sun claps!

Summer's Breath and the Inward Sea

In summer's breath, the world is bright,
Bees play tag while flowers take flight.
I try to sip coconut with a straw,
But it's fighting back in an unusual law!

Pineapples giggle when I walk by,
"Careful, buddy, don't let that slip dry!"
Watermelon smiles hiding in green,
As I accidentally create a fruit scene.

The waves tease me with their foamy glee,
Yanking my toes, as they run to flee.
Summer dresses a spectacle grand,
But I always end up across the sand!

As dusk descends, a firefly show,
Guiding my path like a glowing disco.
If laughter be the treasure of the day,
I'm rich beyond measure, hip-hip-hooray!

The Tango of Tides and Terrain

In flip-flops they glide, what a sight,
The beach bunnies dance, oh what delight.
With sand stuck to toes, they twirl and sway,
While seagulls mock them in their own way.

A crab joins the fun, snaps to the beat,
Dancing sideways, oh, isn't he neat?
They twirl with such joy, what a mess they make,
Roll in the surf, it's a grand mistake.

The sun gives a wink, the waves take a bow,
Dance floor on sand, a bizarrely fun crowd.
Each twist of the tide sends them off course,
A conga line formed by a mischievous horse.

With laughter so loud, they forget the heat,
Grinning like fools, all joy and no defeat.
The tango continues, no end in sight,
With sunburnt backs and smiles, pure delight.

Solstice Stroll Through Paradise

Sunglasses perched, they strut with flair,
Hats twice their size, blowing in the air.
Ice cream drips down, a rainbow of mess,
But who cares? They laugh, they love the excess.

Flip-flops squeak loud, a tune of their own,
Walking through blossoms, in gardens overgrown.
Each flower a giggle, each breeze a tease,
Watching the bees dance and plunder with ease.

Sticky with nectar, they waddle and sway,
Sipping on coconuts, oh what a day!
The parade of laughter echoes afar,
As parrots join in, they're the real stars.

Lost in this carnival, giddy and bold,
Every step a whimsy, stories untold.
Sunset creeps in, with a soft, golden hue,
They twirl with the colors, just like they do.

Kisses from a Lavender Sunset

Skies blush and giggle, a ticklish delight,
Waves play hide and seek, under soft twilight.
Laughter erupts as the sun takes a dive,
Bikinis flip-flop, it's how they thrive.

The ocean whispers secrets, all tongue-in-cheek,
With every splash, the funny fish sneak.
Frogs in bow ties croak jokes, quite absurd,
While sunburned tourists, with puns, are stirred.

Lavender clouds tease, a canvas so fine,
Picnics of giggles and glasses of wine.
Each sunset a punchline, a joke draped in gold,
As shadows dance wildly, out of control.

Under this charm, spirits soaring high,
Even the crickets join in, oh my!
They gather together for this silly show,
As night wraps them gently, like soft marshmallow.

Untamed Echoes of the Rainforest

In a jungle so thick, where vines tend to swing,
Monkeys play tag, such a raucous fling.
Leaves whisper secrets, the flowers can tease,
While toucans hoot loudly, a laugh in the breeze.

Frogs in tuxedos leap high on a quest,
While sloths hang around, never in a rush, just rest.
Giggling through canopies, a wild parade,
As critters conspire, their plans well laid.

Caterpillars chatter, with dreams to take flight,
Chasing the butterflies, what a silly sight!
Swing from the branches, let the glittering rain,
Fall like confetti, all silly and strange.

Under the cover of emerald green,
A symphony of laughter, a cacophony seen.
No worries of time, they dance through the night,
In the wild world of joy, all feels just right.

Flames of the Setting Sun

The sky's on fire, what's that I see?
A coconut falling, aiming for me!
The sun's a griller, oh will it fry?
I dodge and I weave, oh my, oh my!

The lizards are dancing, tails in a twist,
While I'm over here, lost in the mist.
A parrot squawks jokes in the heat of the day,
He says, 'Hey buddy, try not to sway!'

Serenade of the Monsoon Wind

The clouds conspire, brewing a tease,
A sprinkle of rain, oh please, oh please!
Umbrellas turned inside out, what a sight,
As we jog down the street, giggling in fright.

Puddles are jumping, a splash here and there,
I'm soaked to the bone, but don't really care.
The wind sings a tune, a silly little hum,
'Come dance in the downpour, you're never too dumb!'

The Cacao Grove's Lullaby

In the cacao grove, the monkeys conspire,
Swinging from branches, fueled by desire.
Those beans have a plan, oh what a delight,
To make chocolate dreams, as sweet as a bite!

Beneath the thick canopy, secrets unfold,
With laughter and giggles, both precious and bold.
A cocoa clown leaps, in a comical pose,
'Eat all of my beans, let's see how it goes!'

Quest for Currents and Calm

A paddle in hand, I set off with glee,
To float on a river that's calling to me.
But what's that I see? A frog wearing a crown!
He quips, 'You'd best stay afloat, or you'll drown!'

I navigate waters that swirl with a laugh,
Dodging the drips from the green leafy staff.
The current is playful, behaves like a child,
'You're up for a splash, aren't you?' it smiled!

The Dance of Fireflies at Dusk

Fireflies twinkle like lost stars,
In my yard, they swish and sway.
I trip on grass, bump my knee,
They laugh; oh, what a display!

In the twilight, they begin to tease,
With their glow, they lead the way.
Caught in a clumsy jig of joy,
I follow, but I'm the menu today!

A frog joins in with a ribbit cheer,
While the moon peeks out in glee.
I still can't dance, but oh dear,
At least the bugs think I'm fancy!

With squawks from night, my footwear's torn,
A firefly gives me a stern look.
Next to them, I'm a bumbling fool,
But tonight, I'll dance like I'm in a book!

Mystic Nights and Daydreams

Night falls and my thoughts start to drift,
The dreams take over with a mighty twist.
A parrot sings in a bewildering tune,
I snicker loudly, inspired by the moon.

The coconut tree whispers secrets in the dark,
As I sway like a ship, a reluctant lark.
Here comes a lizard, striking a pose,
I roll my eyes; what a way to amuse!

Drifting dreaming on my porch swing,
Crickets perform their rave-like thing.
Sipping lemonade, it's running low,
Did I drop my last slice? Oh no, oh no!

Just as I dream of penguins in socks,
Reality nudges; it's time for the locks.
With fuzzy night visions, I giggle and grin,
A night well spent, let the fun begin!

Tides Beneath the Sweltering Moon

The ocean rolls like a lazy cat,
Underneath the moon, it yawns and splats.
I chase the waves, lose my flip-flop,
The tides laugh back, they never stop.

A crab winks at me, all smug and sly,
With its sideways dance, I heave a sigh.
Seagulls squawk; I swear they giggle,
As I trip over sand, doing the wiggle.

Shells whisper tales from the sandy shore,
The sand gets hot; that's quite a chore.
But with each splash, my spirits rise,
In this sea of fun, I'm the biggest surprise!

I leap and fumble, rough and wild,
In this ocean ballet, oh what a child!
The moon beams down, a dazzling tune,
And the tides keep dancing, beneath the moon.

Colors of Chaos: A Tropical Palette

In a garden bright with colors awry,
Where strawberries giggle and tomatoes lie.
I fling my paintbrush, try to be bold,
But end up with a canvas that's a sight to behold.

Blue here, green there, a splash of pink,
It feels like art is missing the link.
A monkey swings by, gives me the eye,
My masterpiece, he'd surely deny!

The flowers all gawk; their petals shake,
I can hear them whisper, 'For goodness' sake!'
Yet somehow, in laughter, I find my bliss,
As bees buzz around—could it be art's kiss?

I stand in the chaos, covered in hue,
With each swipe, dreams morph and skew.
In this tropical mess, I declare with pride,
Beauty can bloom from even the wildest ride!

Sheltering Under the Hibiscus

The sun blazes bright, like a torch in July,
My hat's a sweat lodge, oh why oh why!
The hibiscus is swooning, a flower has flair,
Yet I'm stuck in the shade, applying my spare.

The breeze does a tango with my loose shirt,
While sipping a drink that's more juice than dirt.
The splashes of laughter, the giggles that ring,
Who's swimming in pools? I'm just here with my fling.

An ant on my foot, it's joining the dance,
I'd swat it away, but it's got the right stance!
Margaritas are plentiful, laughs are aplenty,
Look at me now, I'm the king of the empty!

So, here's to this shade, where we burble and chat,
With flies buzzing 'round like they're part of the spat.
As laughter erupts and the sun starts to fade,
I'll never complain, in this funny charade.

Vibrations of a Flaming Sunset

Sunset's a party; the colors take charge,
Like a painter gone wild—a canvas at large.
The flamingo in pink throws a cocktail for me,
But I'm spilling my drink; oh, where can it be?

The clouds are all giggling; the seagulls all cheer,
While I try to keep calm with a splash of cold beer.
The shadows grow longer, but I'm still in my flip,
Tripping over my laughter while doing a dip.

The palm trees are whispering secrets to night,
As I catch my reflection—what a comical sight!
We dance on the beach while the sand takes a bite,
Swaying like kelp, I'm a soft, silly kite.

With the ocean as DJ, the waves sing their tune,
And we wiggle and jiggle beneath the bright moon.
So let's toast to this chaos, where fun meets the sun,
With laughter as currency, we're richer, by fun!

Treasures of the Sunlit Shore

The treasures here sparkle like diamonds so bright,
But I trip on a shell—what a glorious sight!
Sandcastles rise high; mine looks more like a lump,
The tide rolls it over; oh, what a sad thump!

Buckets and spades are scattered about,
But my bucket's now serving as a hat, there's no doubt.
Children are squealing; they're racing the breeze,
While I'm chasing crabs that have found my bare knees.

A seagull steals fries like an old-timey thief,
I shout in protest, but it's too late, oh grief!
With laughter contagious, we all pause to see,
The seagull divides with my old sandwich spree.

So here's to the chaos and fun in the sun,
With treasures misplaced, this goofy life's won.
Each grain of the sand is a moment we share,
As laughter and memories blend into the air.

Lament of the Lapping Waves

The waves come a-lapping, a rhythm to tease,
But my toes in the water say 'Ouch!' with great ease.
Each splash makes me giggle, a playful routine,
Though I'm caught, like a marionette, it seems.

The sun tells me tales of adventures at sea,
While I drown in my thoughts, sipping cold herbal tea.
The laughter-like bubbles rise high in the air,
Who needs an ocean when I've got this chair?

Flipping and flopping like a fish out of place,
I wave every passerby with a strange, goofy grace.
A crab scuttles by, he's on a lone quest,
"Who could be sillier? Me or the rest?"

So here by the shore, where the waves kiss the sand,
We chant silly verses, all perfectly planned.
In this mellow lament, we're merry, not blue,
Life's laughter in waves, such a delightful view!

Embers of the Tropical Sun

The sun was hot, no doubt at all,
My ice cream melted, took a fall.
Birds chirped loud, in feathered glee,
While I just sweated like a flea.

Flip-flops squeaked upon the sand,
Like little crabs that dance and scamp.
A beach ball soared, then hit my head,
I laughed so hard, I nearly fled.

Palm leaf fans, I waved with flair,
But all they did was mess my hair.
A coconut, my drink of choice,
Spilled all over—oh, rejoice!

At dusk, I grinned, the heat was tamed,
The fireflies danced as the crickets claimed.
For when the heat became too grand,
We all just chuckled—life's unplanned!

Glint of the Stardust Shore

The moonlight sparkled on the waves,
While crabs pinched toes, oh, how they'd rave!
A starfish waved, it tried to dance,
I found it funny, it lost its chance.

Sandcastles rose with much delight,
Then fell apart—it was quite the sight.
Seagulls squawked like they owned the view,
I threw them chips—they flew, oh boo!

A dolphin jumped to steal the show,
My friends all cheered, said, 'Go, go, go!'
But while they watched, one tripped and fell,
Into the tide—oh, what a smell!

As evening fell, we shared a grin,
The ocean's life, it drew us in.
With laughter ringing, hearts so sure,
We basked beneath that glinting lure!

Vibrant Echoes of Heartbeats

A parrot squawked in vibrant hues,
I tried to mimic, but lost my shoes.
My friend just giggled, dropped her drink,
And in the chaos, we failed to think.

Tropical fruits—oh, what a feast!
But I slipped on papaya, what a beast!
The pineapple crown sat wild on me,
I laughed and danced—great sight to see!

With salsa beats that shook the night,
We danced like goofballs, lost in flight.
The fireflies blinked, kept time with song,
And we just knew we couldn't go wrong.

Echoes of laughter filled the air,
As friends fell down with a silly flair.
In vibrant hues, we made our mark,
Together in joy, like a tropical spark!

The Thrum of Tropical Existence

In the jungles loud with vibrant cries,
Monkeys swung by with mischief in their eyes.
We tried to keep pace, but they were fleet,
So we just sat, and admitted defeat.

With every step, a squish or slide,
The dampened earth became our guide.
And just when we thought we'd crossed it slick,
A mud pit came—we didn't pick!

The night arrived, the stars would shine,
But mosquitoes buzzed, they crossed the line.
We swatted and danced, oh what a mess,
In this tropical haven, nothing's less!

As laughter echoed, we found our place,
Embracing chaos—with a smile on our face.
For in this rhythm, so wild and free,
The thrum of existence—the key to glee!

Sipping Beauty from a Coconut

A coconut winks, oh so bold,
Its milk is sweet, the sun like gold.
I sip and dream of island fare,
Yet drink it slow without a care.

With every gulp, my laughter grows,
The beach chair sways, how funny it goes!
A seagull steals my snack with glee,
I toast to him, my coconut spree!

The sunburned tourists vie for shade,
I wave my drink, in shade I wade.
I crack a joke; a crab walks by,
He pinches me—oh, my oh my!

So cheers to life with a coconut grin,
Where fun and sun are twin brothers' kin.
With sand in my toes, I laugh so bright,
Let the coconut party last all night!

Reflections in Tropical Rain

The sky is gray, a fickle tease,
Yet in the warmth, I dance with ease.
The puddles laugh, they splash my shoes,
I tickle raindrops, what a ruse!

Umbrellas open like a grand parade,
Each one spins like a brightly clad mermaid.
The colors swirl, a joyful sight,
As raindrops tango in sheer delight!

A monkey leaps, he does a twist,
I can't resist, I too persist!
With puddles high, my pants are soaked,
But oh, the fun—the giggles provoked!

With thunder claps, the laughter grows,
As rain-soaked friends strike dance poses.
The sky may frown, but hearts are gay,
In tropical rain, we laugh and play!

Canvas of Exotic Dusk

The sky blazes, in colors so bright,
Like a painter who's lost in pure delight.
Palms sway gently, like they know the plot,
As the sun bids farewell—what a whimsical spot!

Dinner is served, a feast of delight,
With bugs that buzz, yet I'll dine tonight.
The laughter flows like tropical breeze,
While I dodge a few—seriously, please!

Flamboyant sunsets, we toss silly names,
In the sky's canvas, no one's to blame.
I trip on sand, causing a scene,
But the crab clapped first, oh what a queen!

So let's toast to dusk, where laughter ignites,
In this colorful world, we share wild sights.
With every giggle, we smear the scene,
In an artist's dream, let's keep it green!

Dive into the Serpent's Pool

In the pool where mischief bubbles up high,
I leap like a fish, yet I'm a fly guy.
The waves splash back, saying hello,
With each cannonball, my antics glow!

A serpent's tail swirls; what a sight!
But it's just my buddy—oh, what a fright!
We giggle and splash like reckless kids,
While dodging those "serpents" under lids.

Every dive sends water spiraling wide,
While I swim with style, there's nowhere to hide.
Yet a rubber shark steals my swim trunks,
Pinching and tugging—oh, the monkey funks!

So, let's dive deep in this silly pool,
Where laughter bubbles and nobody's cruel.
With each wacky splash, we find our groove,
In the water's chaos, we all just move!

Echoes of the Ocean's Embrace

The sun fell in love with the turquoise sea,
But the waves just laughed, 'You can't catch me!'
Crabs put on sunscreen, out in their chairs,
While seagulls plot mischief in beachside glares.

The sandcastles trembled, the tide drew near,
As kids yelled, 'Mom! I think there's a pier!'
But all she could find was a flip-flop snack,
The ocean's a prankster, with laughs on its back.

A dolphin named Dave had a beach ball spree,
While turtles in shades drank their coconut tea.
They'd wager on races, who'd get to the shore,
But everyone knew the waves kept the score.

So under palm shades, in comfort and cheer,
We danced to the rhythm, and tossed back a beer.
In the echoes of laughter, with sandy retreat,
Life's best vacation is light on your feet.

Dance of the Fireflies

Fireflies twinkled like stars on the run,
Whizzing past noses, oh what silly fun!
They laughed and they flashed with their tiny bright lights,
While grasshoppers joined in, making odd bites.

A frog on a lily pad croaked out a tune,
Complaining of traffic that came with the moon.
Butterflies flitted, but tripped on their wings,
As crickets composed a strange symphony sings.

But just as they gathered their merry parade,
The wind gave a shiver, intentions delayed.
The pixies were restless, they wanted to play,
While shadows grew longer, they danced anyway.

In this world of laughter, mistake after jest,
Every vibrant creature laughed hard with the rest.
So join in the frolic, the sparkles ignite,
For magic comes alive twirling wild in the night.

Heat Haze Over Golden Sands

The sunbeam snoozes, while flip-flops squeak,
Sweaty ice cream dribbles, it's quite the peak.
With hats made of palm leaves and shades on our noses,
We giggle at lizards that nobody knows-es.

Sandballs are flying, like cannonballs they soar,
While kids organize battles with rubber galore.
A turtle named Turbo at last breaks his shell,
And dives for the cookie that fell with a yell.

A beach ball's explosion brings giggles galore,
As folks chase the pieces in frantic uproar.
The umbrellas are fighting, oh dear, what a scene,
Each colorful canopy claims a new queen!

In this golden chaos, we savor the heat,
Where laughter is served up on every warm beat.
So come sip your juice, hold your ice cream tight,
In a world where mischief takes center stage tonight.

Passionate Heat and Fading Light

As dusk tiptoes softly with pizza in hand,
The BBQ's crackling, things got out of hand!
With burgers and laughter, the night dances near,
But somehow we lost the ketchup, oh dear!

The fire pit flickers, and marshmallows gleam,
Yet squirrels've declared war, they're stealing our dream.
With ghost stories brewing, we all jump with fright,
While shadows play tricks on our laughter-filled night.

The stars start to twinkle, a wink from above,
While the mosquitoes buzz with a devious love.
We wave at the moon, who's grinning just right,
While all of our plans float away into night.

With bellies all full and dreams still in sight,
We'll cherish these moments, laughing till light.
For friendship's the treasure that glows ever bright,
In the fading warm whispers of laughter and light.

Waves in the Golden Hours

The sun melts like butter spread,
Seagulls plot, a cheeky thread.
Kids run wild, sand in their toes,
Ice cream's dribbled on their nose.

Palm trees sway, a dance routine,
Swaying to a beat unseen.
Laughter echoes, a joyful sound,
As flip-flops fly right off the ground.

Beach ball bounces, chaos reigns,
Someone yells, 'Get off my trains!'
Towels spread like circus dreams,
In this land of sun and beams.

As the waves crash, they tease and play,
"Catch me if you can!" they say.
Good vibes float on salted air,
Here, happiness is everywhere.

Exhale into the Firefly Night

As dusk settles, the laughter grows,
Fireflies dance in sparkly rows.
Nighttime giggles fill the skies,
While shadows chase the moonlit eyes.

Binoculars aimed at the stars,
"Hey look, I see Mars!" from afar.
S'mores stick to fingers and chins,
While stories swirl like firefly spins.

The campfire pops, it cracks, then sighs,
"Who touched my snack?" a voice implies.
Ghosts of gummies haunt the place,
As sugar high brings smiles to face.

With yawns and jokes, the night rolls on,
Under the gaze of a million dawns.
Sleep beckons, but laughter's still bright,
In the air, it's pure delight.

Shadows Flickering on the Dune

By the dunes, the shadows weave,
Sandcastles built with a cheeky reprieve.
Sand in hair, lost flip-flops roam,
One kid claims, "This is my home!"

Footprints trail like a giggly race,
Sandy cheeks adorn each face.
A kite gets stuck in a coconut high,
"Help me!" it cries, as we all sigh.

The sunset brings a golden glow,
Sunscreen still smells like yesterday's show.
Chasing pigeons seems like a dream,
With ice creams melting in the scheme.

As night falls, the stars peek through,
A dance of shadows, a playful crew.
We laugh and toss our cares away,
Join the merry in a sunset ballet.

Rapture of the Unbroken Sea

The ocean whispers a goofy tune,
Surfboards dance like spoons in June.
Waves crash softly, a foamy smile,
Riding high, we forget the while.

With a splash, someone takes a dive,
"Hey, what's up?"—their laughter's alive.
Seashells roll like dice in the sand,
Treasure hunters formed a merry band.

A crab walks by, a scuttling clown,
With pinchers raised, it wears a frown.
"Sharing is caring!" We all proclaim,
As laughter shakes the sandy frame.

When stars peek out from ocean's arms,
We count them all with silly charms.
In this rapture, joy takes flight,
Chasing dreams through the ocean's light.

Sunkissed Reverie

The sun is a chef, cooking up rays,
With squirrels in shades, enjoying the plays.
They sip on cool drinks, with little umbrellas,
While I sweat like a pig, chasing my fellas.

My skin's now a toast, golden and crisp,
As I chase down a lizard with the fastest grip.
The beach ball's revolt, it floats from my grasp,
Dancing with waves, oh how they gasp!

Seagulls are laughing, they steal my snack,
I yell, "Hey, that's mine! Come give it back!"
But they fly off, giggling, in a feathered parade,
While I flop on the sand, feeling betrayed.

As the sun sets low, I ponder my fate,
A burnt marshmallow, on a sunburnt plate.
Yet with friends around, laughter mixed in,
We toast to our sunburns, let the fun begin!

Lush Whispers of the Jungle

In the jungle so thick, where the monkeys swing,
I thought I could hide, but they laugh and they sing.
With vines like a maze, I fumble and trip,
Getting caught in the arms of a slippery grip.

The toucans stare down from the branches so proud,
As I wipe off my sweat, feeling lost in the crowd.
A snake slithers by, with a wink and a shake,
I say, "Not today, buddy! I'm out for a break!"

Frogs in the mud, doing a funny jig,
While I trip on a root, oh man, it's so big!
They croak and they ribbit, forming a choir,
As I stumble and mumble, "What's that? A new hire?"

Under towering trees, the shadows grow long,
With critters all laughing, I'm sure they are wrong.
But as dusk settles down, with a smile on my face,
I'll dance with the frogs, in this wild, crazy place!

Shadows Dance Under Canopy

Beneath the green giants, the shadows do twist,
I step on a beetle, oh no, I can't resist!
The critter grows loud, giving me quite the fright,
As I hop like a deer, in the dim fading light.

The fireflies flicker, like stars in the night,
But they buzz 'round my head, it's quite the sight!
I swat like a madman, oh, get off my nose!
These blinky little guys bring friends to my woes.

With laughter and giggles from friends all around,
We join in a conga, marching unbound.
But the floor is all sticky, with mud and some leaves,
And we slip like we're skating, oh, no one believes!

As the laughter erupts, the stars start to glow,
In this jungle of dreams, we let all joy flow.
With shadows that linger, and jokes we can't quit,
We'll dance 'til we're dizzy, oh, isn't life a hit?

Sunbeams on the Rafting River

On a raft made of laughter, we plunge with a splash,
As I nearly fall over, oh what a crash!
The sun's like a spotlight, shining on me,
While fishes below giggle and swim wild and free.

Paddles are flailing, like dancers in cheer,
A honk from a duck makes us howl with a sneer.
As we zig and we zag, the current takes hold,
We should've paid heed to the tale we were told.

But the thrill of the ride, oh how it excites,
Our tubes roll away, what a laugh in our sights!
With a splash like a cannon, we whoop and we scream,
While sunbeams above weave us into a dream.

As we drift down the river, with water and sun,
This silly adventure has been so much fun.
So here's to the giggles, the splashes, the glee,
In the embrace of bright rays, we're all wild and free!

Mirage of the Midnight Jungle

In the jungle's swelter, I spy a light,
A disco ball twirling, not quite right.
Monkeys in sunglasses, grooving with glee,
While parrots sing songs of pure jubilee.

Beneath the palm fronds, the party's a blast,
An iguana DJ spinning tunes fast.
The toucans are dancing, it's quite the scene,
In this sweltering jungle, we're living the dream.

Lizards in tuxedos, who knew they would dress?
While frogs keep on hopping, I must confess.
With a drink in my hand, I lounge in style,
This midnight jungle party, I could stay a while.

But wait! A mirage, am I losing my mind?
In this shimmering heat, I stand unconfined.
Reality blurs in the warm, humid mist,
I join in the fun; who could resist?

Fragrant Tropics in Full Bloom

Floral aromas dancing through the air,
A coconut caught in a tropical snare.
Bees in sombreros, buzzing a tune,
While a monkey sneaks snacks, a real buffoon.

Bamboo windchimes playing a jazzy beat,
Laughter erupts from my sandy seat.
The sunflowers gossip, sharing their dreams,
While flamingos pose with glittery beams.

Coconut drinks served with tiny umbrellas,
A parrot's wisecracks, oh, such a fella!
Hibiscus cheerleaders, waving their fronds,
As I sip and soak up these tropic fond bonds.

In this fragrant paradise, time's lost its pace,
We dance and we joke, a super fun chase.
With friends all around, how can one feel blue?
These blossoms are blooms, and we're merry too!

Reverie in the Shade

I lay in the shade, my thoughts taking flight,
A hammock sways gently, it feels just right.
The chimes of the wind tease my sunny dreams,
While monkeys concoct their mischievous schemes.

Coconut crabs in their tiny parade,
Marching with flair, in the cool, leafy glade.
The sun plays peek-a-boo through leafy green,
As I crack up at ants in a comical scene.

Palm trees stifle giggles, rustling their leaves,
While a sloth takes selfies, oh what a tease!
Could paradise get any wackier than this?
A day in the shade is pure pure bliss!

So I float on my thoughts, chilled drink in my hand,
In this funny forest, life's perfectly planned.
With a wink and a grin, I'm lost in this flow,
Reveling in laughter, feeling the glow!

Cascades of Color and Heat

Colors cascade like a rainbow on fire,
As I sizzle and giggle, I can't help but tire.
The peacocks are strutting, all glam and flair,
While a turtle's breakdancing, unaware of the glare.

Sunsets explode, melting into delight,
As fireflies flicker to welcome the night.
The cactus throws punches, oh what a sight,
While iguanas in shades sip drinks with great might.

With laughter as bright as the sun's golden rays,
We frolic in colors, in outlandish ways.
The orchids can't help but blush in the heat,
As we dance to the rhythm of this quirky beat.

So grab your sombrero, come join the parade,
In this vibrant oasis where memories are made.
With cascades of color swirling all around,
We find humor and joy in this tropical playground!

www.ingramcontent.com/pod-product-compliance
Lightning Source LLC
Chambersburg PA
CBHW072215070526
44585CB00015B/1346